Contents

What do shopkeepers do?   4

Things to make and do

Different kinds of shops   6

Take a trip to the shops   8

Let's play shops!   10

Stocking and stacking   12

Play the part

The birthday present   14

Shiny shoes and football boots   16

My robot has broken down!   18

Come dine with me   20

Come dine with me (continued)   22

Glossary   24

Index   24

What do shopkeepers do?

Shops are the places where we go to buy the things we need and want. Shops are run and looked after by shopkeepers.

Shopkeepers have long and busy days. They **order** in the **goods** that are sold in the shop. Then they **display** these goods so the **customers** can see them.

To play the part of a shopkeeper you can dress up in a uniform. The uniform could be a top with trousers or skirt in the same colour, or a smart shirt and tie. If you are playing a shopkeeper selling foodstuff then you could wear an apron. Many shopkeepers also wear name badges.

During **opening hours**, shopkeepers help the customers.

Different kinds of shops

Shops are everywhere! Small villages may only have a **grocery** or **post office**. Towns might have lots of different shops such as pet shops and bookshops. In cities there are **shopping centres** with lots of shops under one roof.

Some shops sell just one kind of thing. Bakeries sell bread, buns and cakes. Chemists sell things to make you look and feel well. You can get medicine, make-up, shampoo and toothpaste there. What other kinds of shops do you know?

Collect items for your shop

Think about the kind of shop you would like to set up. Start collecting items for your shop. Look out for old tins, packets, plastic containers and boxes. To set up a shoe shop collect a variety of old shoes and shoe boxes.

Take a trip to the shops

Next time you visit the shops have a good look around you. Take time to look at how things are displayed in different shops. When you're inside a shop, find out whether items are put on shelves or hung up on racks.

While you're shopping watch what shopkeepers do. Listen to how they help customers. Do the shopkeepers wrap up the items or put them in bags?

Make your own shop sign

On your shopping trip you will have seen lots of different shop signs. You can make your own fantastic shop sign.

Choose the kind of shop sign you would like to make. If you pick a bakery then you could make the sign in the shape of a big cake or draw a cake on it.

1 Cut the cardboard into the shape you would like your sign to be.

2 Draw the name of your shop in pencil. Try out different styles of writing. You could use all capital letters.

3 When you are happy with the name, you can draw pictures or patterns around the letters.

4 Colour in the letters, pictures and patterns using paints or felt-tip pens.

5 Carry on decorating the sign as you wish. Use glue and add glitter, tissue paper or anything else you want to decorate your sign.

6 To hang your sign up, use a hole punch to make a hole in the sign and thread a piece of string through it.

Let's play shops!

When you play the part of a shopkeeper you need a **shop counter**. The most important item on the counter is the **till**. There are plenty of toy tills to choose from. Some have a **scanner** that bleeps when you scan items. Some tills also have a **chip and pin machine** for paying by **debit card**.

scanner

chip and pin machine

Set up the shop counter

1. Make a table into a counter. Cover the table with coloured paper.

2. Stick the shop sign to the front of your counter with sticky tape or hang it up on the wall.

3. Arrange the till, notebook, telephone and pens neatly on the counter.

4. Sort the toy money into the till.

5. Arrange a few items for sale on the counter.

6. Cut out some brightly coloured card and make a **special offer** sign for your goods.

7. Make sure you have bags and sticky tape ready for packing.

You will need:

- ★ Shop sign
- ★ A table
- ★ A toy till or small box
- ★ Toy money
- ★ Telephone
- ★ Notebook
- ★ Pens
- ★ Large sheet of coloured paper
- ★ Bags
- ★ Coloured card
- ★ Sticky tape

SPECIAL OFFER! BUY 2 BOOKS GET 1 FREE!

STAR BUY ½ · PRICE ON ALL TOYS !!

BUY 1 TIN GET 1 FREE

DAN & MAYA'S GROCERY SHOP

Stocking and stacking

Shopkeepers display their goods so the customers can see them. At a grocery shop packets and tins are stacked on shelves. Fruit and vegetables are displayed in baskets or boxes. Chilled food is found in fridges and frozen food in freezers. Sweets and ice creams are often put next to the shop counter.

Set up your own shop display

Cover tables or boxes with coloured paper or use some real shelves. Arrange your items for sale on the tables. Write some prices for the goods on sticky labels and stick them in places where they can be seen.

Make your own ice creams and stand

You will need:

★ Small cardboard box
★ Three cardboard rolls
★ Thin yellow card
★ Sheets of tissue paper
★ Yellow sponge cleaner
★ Brown and red modelling clay
★ Paint
★ Sticky tape
★ Scissors
★ Glue

1 To make the ice cream stand take a small cardboard box and paint 'ICE CREAM' on the outside.

2 Stick three cardboard rolls to the inside of the front of the box using sticky tape.

3 To make the ice cream cones, roll the thin yellow card into cones. Use sticky tape to secure the cone in place.

4 To make the scoops of ice cream scrunch up the tissue paper into balls and glue onto the cones.

5 Cut the yellow sponge cleaner into triangles to make wafers.

6 Roll tiny bits of brown modelling clay to make chocolate sprinkles.

7 Roll red modelling clay into balls to make cherries.

8 Glue the wafers, sprinkles and cherries to the ice cream.

9 Place the cones in the cardboard rolls in the ice cream stand.

You have set the scene and made some props. Now you can begin to play the part of a shopkeeper in these role plays.

The birthday present

Play the parts of a shopkeeper at a bookshop, and a customer who wants to buy a birthday present for a friend. You should be able to find lots of books at home or school to stock this shop!

 SHOPKEEPER: *(behind the shop counter)* Good morning. Can I help you?

 FINN: I'd like to buy a birthday present for my friend.

 SHOPKEEPER: The children's books are over there. *(points to the shelves)*

FINN: Great! *(looks at the books)* I think he'd like something about monsters.

SHOPKEEPER: How about this one! *(shows a book with monsters on the cover)*

FINN: *(flicks through the book)* Oh dear, that's too scary.

 SHOPKEEPER: Well, this one here is funny. *(shows him a picture book about monsters)*

 FINN: *(laughs at the pictures)* It's brilliant. How much is it?

 SHOPKEEPER: It's £6…

WHAT HAPPENS NEXT?

You can decide what happens next in this scene. Below are some fun ideas that you could try acting out using your own words. Then have a go at making up your own scenes.

1 Finn decides to buy the book. He pays for the book using his debit card.

2 Finn cannot afford this book. He asks the shopkeeper to help him find something cheaper.

3 Finn likes the book so much he buys two copies – one for his friend and one for himself. The shopkeeper scans the books and tells Finn they will cost £12. Finn gives her £15. Can you work out the change the shopkeeper needs to give Finn?

Shiny shoes and football boots

In this scene you can take it in turns being the customers and the shopkeeper in a shoe shop.

 JESS: I like these shiny gold shoes. Do you have my size please?

 SHOPKEEPER: We'd better measure your feet.

 **SHOPKEEPER:** You're a size 12. I'll check if we have them… *(Shopkeeper returns with the shoes and Jess tries them on.)*

 JESS: *(walking around, trying them out for size)* Oh, aren't they lovely?

HARRY: *(dashes into the shop)* I'm in a rush. Do you have a pair of size 12 football boots please?

 SHOPKEEPER: Here, try these on.

(Shopkeeper helps Harry try on the boots.)

 HARRY: These are good – I'll take them!

 JESS: These shoes are perfect – I'll take them!

WHAT HAPPENS NEXT?

You can decide what happens next in this scene. Below are some fun ideas that you could try acting out using your own words. Then have a go at making up your own scenes.

1 The shopkeeper gets in a muddle. He puts the shiny shoes in the football boots box and the football boots in the shiny shoes box. Jess and Harry have to bring the shoes back.

2 The shopkeeper checks Harry's boots and says they're too tight. He finds him a pair that fit perfectly. Harry pays in a hurry because he's off to play football straight away!

3 Jess can't decide between a gold pair or a silver pair. She asks other customers in the shop to help her choose.

My robot has broken down!

Play the parts of a shopkeeper and customer in a toyshop. You can use your own toys as goods in the toyshop.

 MRS JAMES: *(standing behind shop counter)* Hello, can I help you?

 FELIX: I bought this robot last week, but it's not working anymore.

MRS JAMES: Oh dear, do you have the **receipt**?

 FELIX: Yes, here it is! *(Felix gives Mrs James the receipt)*

 **MRS JAMES:** Good – now let me have a look at that poor old robot!

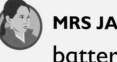 **MRS JAMES:** Maybe the batteries need changing.

(Mrs James puts new batteries in the robot, but it still doesn't work.)

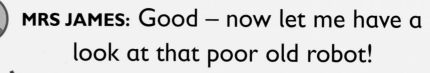

18

FELIX: See, it has broken hasn't it?

 MRS JAMES: Well, let's get a screwdriver and look inside…

WHAT HAPPENS NEXT?

You can decide what happens next in this scene. Below are some fun ideas that you could try acting out using your own words. Then have a go at making up your own scenes.

1 Mrs James tightens up a loose screw in the robot. Hey presto! The robot is working!

2 Felix tells Mrs James that he doesn't want to keep the robot. He has the receipt and would like a full refund.

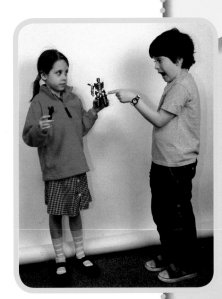

3 Mrs James can't get the robot working and damages it even more. She tells Felix he can exchange the robot for a different toy. Felix exchanges the robot for a shark. The shark costs £5 less so Mrs James gives him some money back.

Come dine with me

Imagine you are going shopping for a barbecue you are going to have. Play the parts of customers and shopkeepers at a grocery shop.

 DAN: *(stacking shelves)* Good morning, nice to see you again.

 MAYA: *(standing behind the counter)* How can we help today?

 JIM: Well, Lila and I are having a barbecue tonight.

LILA: So we're going to needs lots of sausages!

DAN: Better than Best Sausages are on special offer this week – just £1.50 a pack.

JIM: Smashing! We'll have four packs please.

LILA: Oh, we need a basket. *(Lila picks up a toy basket)* What else is on the shopping list Jim?

 JIM: *(Jim looks at the shopping list)* Let's see… bread rolls, cheese and tomatoes.

 MAYA: These bread rolls are still warm. *(Maya points to the bread rolls)*

 JIM: Lovely, let's have ten!

(Jim counts out ten rolls, puts them in a bag and then into the basket)

 JIM: Mmmm, this is my favourite cheese.

(Jim gets some cheese from the fridge and puts it in the basket)

(continued over page)

21

Come dine with me

(continued)

 LILA: These tomatoes look juicy.
(Lila weighs the amount of tomatoes she needs on the scales and pops them in a brown paper bag)

 MAYA: Is that everything?

 JIM: Let's have an ice cream, too.
(Jim points at the ice creams on the stand)

 LILA: Oh yes! But can we afford one?

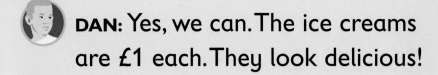

DAN: Yes, we can. The ice creams are £1 each. They look delicious!

LILA: OK, let's pay.

MAYA: *(Maya scans all the items)* Let's see – that will be £20.50 including the ice creams please!

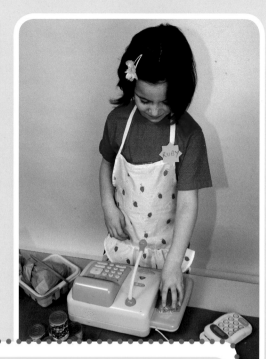

WHAT HAPPENS NEXT?

You can decide what happens next in this scene. Below are some fun ideas that you could try acting out using your own words. Then have a go at making up your own scenes.

1 Lila looks in her purse and finds she only has £20. Lila and Jim put something back so they can afford the ice creams.

2 Jim and Lila remember they haven't bought anything for pudding. They ask Dan and Maya for their suggestions.

3 Maya packs the shopping into carrier bags. But, as Lila and Jim are leaving the shop one of the bags splits. Jim treads and skids on one of the fallen tomatoes and drops his ice cream.

GLOSSARY

chip and pin machine A device used in shops to take a payment from a customer's debit card.

customer A person who is buying goods.

debit card A small plastic card which transfers money from you bank account when you make a purchase.

display An arrangement of goods in a shop, designed to attract customers' attention.

goods Things for sale.

grocery A shop selling food and household supplies.

opening hours The times of the day that a shop is open.

order Ask for something to be sent to you.

post office A shop where you can buy stamps and post letters and parcels.

receipt A piece of paper that proves you have bought something.

scanner A device that reads the barcodes of goods and tells the shopkeeper the price the customer has to pay.

shop counter The desk where goods are sold in a shop.

shopping centre A big building that contains many shops.

special offer Special offers are goods offered at a lower price than normal.

till A box in a shop where money is kept.

INDEX

bakery 7, 9
bookshop 6, 14–15

chemist 7
counter 10, 11, 17, 18, 20
customers 4, 5, 8, 12, 14, 16, 17, 20

debit card 10, 15
displays 4, 8, 12

grocery 6, 12, 20–23

ice cream stand 13, 22

money 15, 19, 23

receipt 18, 19
role play 14–23

shoe shop 7, 16–17
shopping bags 11, 23
shopping baskets 11, 21
shop sign 9, 11
special offers 11, 20

till 10, 11
toyshop 9, 18–19

uniform 5